Crazy Faith

Earl Francis Palmer

ISBN: 978-0-9852481-4-7

Printed in the United States of America
Published through Lulu Enterprise, Inc, Raleigh, N.C
www.lulu.com

Acknowledgements

There are so many people that assisted me in one way or the other to make this book possible. To my family-my wife of over 36 years, Maria, for her continual support and encouragement, my son Joshua, and my daughters Rebecca and Rachel.

Also my friend in the Gospel, Apostle Donald Peart, who provided motivation, and oversaw the publishing of this book. Also his two sons, Donald Peart Jr. and Jeshua Peart, for the cover design.

To our Office Administrator, Claudine McFarlane, and my daughters Rachel Palmer and Rebecca Rush, for their tireless effort in putting together the word processing and other correspondence. To my wife Maria Palmer for proofreading; and my Brand New Life Christian Center church family, for allowing me the freedom to demonstrate instances of "Crazy Faith."

Finally, to my brother and friend in the Gospel, Dr. Michael Curry, for his inspiration, belief in our vision, and for "taking a chance" on us. Thank you Dr. Curry, for your labor of love!

Sincerely,
Apostle Earl F. Palmer
Sr. Pastor-Brand New Life Christian Center

Dedication

It is with great joy that I dedicate this book to my Lord and Savior Jesus Christ. I also dedicate it to my loving wife, Maria, my lover, partner in the Ministry, best friend and life companion for over 36 years.

She has motivated, inspired and assisted me in numerous ways in our 36 years of marriage. I thank the Lord for a woman of wisdom, and discretion who is multi-gifted and talented-a scholar and indeed a woman of virtue.

To you, Hon. Thank you so much for your encouragement and for walking alongside me, understanding me when no one else does, as we continue our journey of exercising "Crazy Faith."

Table of Contents

Foreword

Pastor Earl Palmer is a man of vision and faith. He has developed a forward thinking concept of Kingdom Building for his ministry and the people he serves. He writes about the church and the ministry because he understands the profound impact that the church and ministry has on the lives of people.

John Maxwell once said, "when mature, talented, generous humble individuals –called by God to a level of excellence – begin to minister in God's Spirit – churches grow." It is clear in my mind that Pastor Earl Palmer is the model individual that John Maxwell refers to in his statement.

There is no doubt in my mind that you will benefit greatly from reading this insightful book by Pastor Earl Palmer. He is a trusted friend and gifted called servant of God.

Rev. Dr. Michael D. Curry
Senior Lead Pastor
Kendall Community Church of God
Miami, Florida

Introduction
(Crazy Faith)

You might be wondering by now what is "Crazy Faith?" Or why would someone associate the word faith with another word that is usually used to describe someone or something in a very negative manner?

Usually, whenever we imply that someone is crazy, we are really saying all their senses, reason, or faculties are not altogether in their correct order. The Bible describes faith in Hebrews 11:1 as, "... The substance of things hoped for, the evidence of things not seen." Really what this scripture is saying is that one has to operate or act in such a way as to believe that God has already answered their prayers.

Vine's expository dictionary describes "faith" using the following words: "Pistis", which means "firm persuasion", "A conviction based upon the following"; or "to persuade." So "Crazy Faith" is operating or functioning upon hearing the word of God, believing by faith in spite of the present circumstances, or the way things appear to be. "Crazy", because it sometimes requires a behavior or attitude that is contrary to common sense or reasonable thinking and logic. For example, everyone else may be speaking words contrary to what you are presently believing God for, and in fact they might be calling you "crazy." As long as the word of God supports your position and you got that word from the Lord, be encouraged-you are in good company. Rejoice!

That is why Abraham had this testimony in Romans 4:7, "... and **calleth** those things which are not as though they were." Abraham not only believed but he acted on what he believed. Abraham also "called" or spoke the words that the Lord had spoken to him and watched those words come to pass. This leads us to another revelation concerning **"Crazy Faith."**

In Matthew 7:7, we are told to, "ask, and it shall be given you; seek, and ye shall find; knock, and it shall be opened unto you." Notice the progression of, asking, seeking and knocking. Each represents not only action, but each step of action requires more effort on our part. So, "Crazy Faith" not only involves the mind, or thoughts or the Spirit, but also our radical action as well.

Chapter 1
"Crazy Faith": Going Outside the Four Walls

To illustrate Crazy Faith from a practical perspective, let us look at a few of my personal testimonies, where some radical steps were taken that "sensible, logical thinking people", would characterize as foolish and **"crazy."**

I was already attending a fellowship for quite some time. God led me and promoted me from a Sunday School Teacher to a Deacon, then an Elder. I had, and still have, a passion for souls, so I enjoy the work of an Evangelist. However, on a particular Sunday morning as I sat in the Adult Sunday School class, I felt the Spirit of God leading me to go outside the church building. As I struggled with whether this was God or my flesh, I finally went. As I obeyed, I distinctly heard the voice of the Lord saying to me, go across the street to a building that was at the time a homeless shelter for families.

The struggle had something to do with what other believers might think, should they observe me leaving a Sunday School class to go "across the street." The pressure of what others might say often stops us from stepping out in faith. Sometimes it is very difficult to explain to others what the Holy Spirit has placed in your heart.

Without knowing what I was supposed to do, I just went. As I walked in the building, the security guard asked me what I wanted. He could not help but notice my "big black Bible" almost hidden under my arm. I quietly asked the Holy Spirit, "What now?"

Next, I found myself saying, "I'm here to teach Bible Study to the residents." To my surprise the security guard quickly responded, "Follow me!" He led me downstairs, which I noticed was almost filled to capacity with men, women, boys and girls; but noticeably more men (which was opposite to the condition of the church which had only a few men).

Jesus commanded us to "Go" in.. Matt.28: 19-20, therefore the word of God supported my actions. To my surprise, the security guard shouted, "Everybody, listen up! Turn the TV off; this man is here to teach Bible Study!" Almost instantly, everybody obeyed, and sat down attentively to hear the Word of God. I taught on John 3:16- I'm sure most people could relate to that scripture.

As the altar call was given, it brought tears to my eyes as these families responded in faith. At the end, I invited them to follow me across the street to the church, and some did. That was the start of a refreshing for that ministry. Some of those that came out of that shelter are Ministers, Deacons, Elders, Evangelists and Pastors today. It is "Crazy Faith" because contrary to conventional thinking, one should not leave a "Sunday School" class to go witnessing.

The shocking reality of that particular experience is that most of the time we tell the unsaved to come to church even if they do not have the "proper church clothes." Some saints need to be prepared before the sinners show up in church. Let's just say, that Sunday morning I assured them they were welcome to come to church with me.

However, I did not "prepare" the church to welcome them as they were. For some saints, it took some time for them to adjust., however, that seems to be typical of most churches. Crazy faith on this occasion took me outside the four walls of the church where the harvest was truly plentiful!

As this book is being written one of the brothers who we used to call brother Wes, is now Minister Wes. One day he came to visit me in my office. As we laughed and remembered the "good old days," he reminded me of that day I walked into the homeless shelter.

As he talked, beaming with the joy of the Lord, he said, "Pastor Palmer I must be honest, on many occasions you would come to visit brothers like Isaac, Calvin, Scottie, and myself. As we sat on the front steps of the building we could see you coming across the street to talk to us about Jesus." Laughing out loud ,he continued, "But the minute we saw you we ran for cover. We were hiding from you, but I must confess because you continued coming to see us we eventually stopped running from you."

All those brothers have served and are still serving God in some form of evangelism. TO GOD BE THE GLORY FOR THE GREAT THINGS HE HAS DONE!

Going outside the "Four Walls", or functioning outside the box, often demands courage. Let's look at the word courage:

Courage is the Hebrew word, "Háeaq," which means literally "to show oneself strong".

Other Hebrew words translated as "courage" are described below.
"Courage"=rúah = "spirit" as in Joshua, 2:11.

Joshua 2:11
*And as soon as we had heard these things, our hearts did melt, neither did there remain any more **courage (lit., spirit)** in any man, because of you: for the LORD your God, he is God in heaven above, and in earth beneath.*

"Courage"="lébah" = "the heart" as in Daniel 11:25

Daniel 11:25
*And he shall stir up his power and his **courage (lit., heart)** against the king of the south with a great army; and the king of the south shall be stirred up to battle with a very great and mighty army; but he shall not stand: for they shall forecast devices against him.*

In addition, the Hebrew word "Ámas" which means to "to be quick" or "alert" exhibits the basic attitude from which courage flows.

Courage is therefore, a quality of the mind, and as such, finds a place among the virtues like wisdom. Its opposite cowardice that is found among the mortal "follies" as referenced in **Eccl. 2:12-13.** *"I turned myself to behold wisdom, and madness, and folly: for what can the man do that cometh after the king? even that which hath been already done. **Then I saw that wisdom excelleth folly,** as far as light excelleth darkness.*

Courage will eventually manifest itself in the believer! In the Old Testament it manifests itself on the battlefields. Those who believe the Lord should "fear not."

Isaiah 41:10
***Fear thou not;** for I am with thee: be not dismayed; for I am thy God: I will strengthen thee; yea, I will help thee; yea, I will uphold thee with the right hand of my righteousness.*

Isaiah 41:13-14

[13] *For I the LORD thy God will hold thy right hand, saying unto thee,* **Fear not;** *I will help thee.* [14] **Fear not,** *thou worm Jacob, and ye men of Israel; I will help thee, saith the LORD, and thy redeemer, the Holy One of Israel.*

Jeremiah 1:8

Be not afraid *of their faces: for I am with thee to deliver thee, saith the LORD.*

Ezekiel 2:6

And thou, son of man, **be not afraid** *of them, neither be afraid of their words, though briers and thorns be with thee, and thou dost dwell among scorpions: be not afraid of their words, nor be dismayed at their looks, though they be a rebellious house.*

The absence of the word from the New Testament is striking. The noun "tharsos" occurs only once in Acts 28:15: "And from thence, when the brethren heard of us, they came to meet us as far as Appii forum, and The three taverns: whom when Paul saw, he thanked God, and took **courage.**"

"Tharsos" means to be "daring," to be "bold," and "to be of good cheer." The ideal for the believer is not just the virtue, but rather a quality of life based on faith in the present Christ. We have victory in every occasion, even in the midst of opposition (1Cor. 16:9).

It takes courage to operate in "Crazy Faith" because as these scriptures imply, you have to be strong, alert, fearless, not afraid of their faces, and bold. The Holy Spirit can help you do all of the above.

Chapter 2
"Crazy Faith": Despise Not the Day of Small Beginnings

"Don't despise small beginnings," ("Crazy Faith": calleth those things that are not as though they were).

In 1992 my family and I were living in Overbrook Farms, Philadelphia. I was then serving as an Elder at a particular church in Philadelphia. I was also working full time as a Mechanical Engineer at a manufacturing plant that required some physical exertion and climbing well devoted stairs.

Early in the morning around 5:00 AM I would and still do take my "power walks." (Only now I use the gym). I'll never forget early one morning as I was walking the Holy Spirit impressed upon me to fast and pray. After sharing this with my wife, I decided to do a seven day complete fast of no food or water for seven days while still working a full time job. The Lord brought me through that fast. During the fast, Genesis 12:1 stayed in my heart; that scripture reads:

"Now the Lord had said unto Abram, get thee out of thy country, and from thy kindred, and from thy father's house, unto a land that I will show thee." That word from the Lord would not leave my mind and heart. I tried to ignore it but I couldn't. The calling of God came to me loud and clear- the birthing of a new ministry. Even the name was new: "BRAND NEW LIFE CHRISTIAN CENTER."

"Crazy Faith" works hand in hand with prayer and fasting. Jesus said, "this kind goeth not out but by prayer and fasting."

Prayer and fasting enable us to exercise "Cazy Faith" and take some risks that we would not normally take. An example of this was about seven years earlier when the Senior Pastor of a fellowship resigned and relocated to another area of the state. As the congregation fasted and prayed another Elder and myself went a little longer in our consecration period.

As we were seeking God's direction concerning who should be the next Pastor, the Holy Spirit spoke to me saying that the other Elder should be the Pastor. This Elder was always busy concerning the house of the Lord. He would fix anything that was broken, even the roof. More importantly, he was a very humble, meek man who the Lord placed alongside his Pastor. I joined that ministry later on.

During the congregational meeting I shared what the Lord had placed on my heart. At that time the congregation was just about to vote on my behalf to be the Pastor. As news came to me I instantly declined and requested that my name not be placed on the ballot, and told them what the Lord said to me.

The congregation accepted and we served joyfully for seven years after that. It was at this point seven years later that I went on the seven day complete fast! Unlike many today, I was not seeking to be a Pastor. I was satisfied with my employment then, newly promoted to the position of Director of Engineering in a manufacturing firm. Becoming a Pastor was the last thing on my mind.

As a matter of fact, my children who are all four years apart in age were not yet in college and tuition was high even then. "Crazy Faith" will allow you to travel or sojourn in areas you never imagined or could not have made for yourself. It will place you on track with God's destiny and purpose for your life.

Remember, when you are walking in "Crazy Faith" you will not have all the answers. If you are waiting for the Lord to reveal the entire plan to you, it will not happen. In most cases, the next step is only revealed as you take the first step!

New opportunities will present themselves to you, as you walk in faith. A series of "small steps" sometimes can lead to significant promotions. In 1Samuel 17:34-37, God **prepared** David for this occasion; for the private victories make possible the public victories.

1 Samuel 17:34-37

34 And David said unto Saul, Thy servant kept his father's sheep, and there came a lion, and a bear, and took a lamb out of the flock: 35 And I went out after him, and smote him, and delivered it out of his mouth: and when he arose against me, I caught him by his beard, and smote him, and slew him. 36Thy servant slew both the lion and the bear: and this uncircumcised Philistine shall be as one of them, seeing he hath defied the armies of the living God. 37David said moreover, The LORD that delivered me out of the paw of the lion, and out of the paw of the bear, he will deliver me out of the hand of this Philistine. And Saul said unto David, Go, and the LORD be with thee.

A **seemingly trivial errand** led to a challenging situation that brought glory to God and recognition to David. Be prepared: you never know when your opportunity will come. A Goliath brings new opportunities.

1 Samuel 17:17-26

Motivation brings you to a whole new level even promotion.
1 Samuel 17:23-26

Obstacles: Courage to face your Goliath will bring a whole series of obstacles; they will present themselves, even before you face your Goliath! Whenever you step out in faith, other people will often put obstacles in your way. David's brother ridiculed him (1 Sam 17:28-31). Saul bluntly told David, "You are not able" (1 Sam 17:33). But note what David first said to Saul in verse 32: "And David said to Saul, let no man's heart fail because of him; **thy servant will go and fight with this Philistine.**"

Chapter 3
"Crazy Faith": Trading Familiar with Unfamiliar

"Crazy Faith" will lead you into the realm of the unknown. My wife and I along with our three children were serving at a fellowship in Philadelphia. There was no animosity, resentment, bitterness, or jealousy concerning the Pastors now in place. My wife and I were Elders, at that time serving those under shepherds for seven years. We served the first Pastor of that fellowship for eight years. First we shared with the Pastors of that fellowship, then the Board of Elders the Lord's calling on my life to start a fellowship, and receiving their approval, it was now time to inform the congregation of our decision. We were very careful that we did not cause a "church split." I hate "church splits" and still do.

I distinctly told the congregation that they were forbidden to come with us. We did not want any member from the congregation to leave because of us. So, as an Elder then, I told them publicly and privately to stay and support their Pastors.

Even after much pleading with them, later on a husband and wife, a mother and daughter, and another older lady preferred to go and insisted that they were leaving that fellowship anyway. In the end, we could not keep them from joining with us as they were adamant about joining our newly found congregation. It should be noted however, that when God's call came to me, the only members that I knew I had then were my wife and our three children.

So, that Sunday morning we informed the congregation, gave them a date when we would be leaving; and subsequently served our time there. At that time we left peacefully, without any incident. That church family was just like our own family. Many of our friends and our children's friends were there. We developed many years of relationships and were very comfortable.

Now to move into an area of the "unknown" was not easy to handle. Many tears were shed, and along with the tears came loneliness and isolation. In fact, God called us alone. It was a place in God that was very difficult to deal with. Some things are not worth mentioning; but overall it's fair to say that was a very trying time.

The unfamiliar can also be like a Goliath in your life in facing the unknown. Jesus wants you to take courage and conquer your Goliath. Run towards your oppositions like David ran towards Goliath and defeated the giant. Use the past victories the Lord has done for you as motivation to face your fear. Take courage and fight!

1Samuel 17:34-37 and verses 39 – 40.

In some cases the familiar is preferable; as in this particular case with David. Here he used a "sling-shot"; Saul's sword proved to be too cumbersome, it was unfamiliar to David, but notice that David had not proved it.

Ultimately, we have to walk in the Spirit and allow the Holy Spirit to show us when we need to trade "a familiar with an unfamiliar", or take that risk.

Chapter 4
"Crazy Faith": Failure as an Ingredient

The fear of failure will prevent you from trying or trusting God. The steps of faith sometimes include what I call failure. Abraham experienced this type of failure (delayed obedience) on his way to experiencing successful faith. God gave Abraham three commandments. Abraham obeyed one-the first one. He left his country. However, he failed to obey the last two commandments. Instead of separating himself from his kindred, that is, Terah his father and Lot his nephew, both went with him. Terah means "delay" and points to the fact that Abraham's family delayed his obedience to God's directive. (Genesis 12:1, 4-6).

So, Abraham failed in obeying God's commands. Yet Abraham is known for his faith towards God. Often we fall short of obtaining our miracle only because we experience some form of failure. If you are going to operate in "Crazy Faith", then at some point you will experience failure. For example, our children remember our faith ventures in believing God for our first house. On numerous occasions we confessed, "This is the house the Lord has for us", then we stepped out on faith, and nothing happened. In fact, our children finally got "a word from the Lord" themselves; from then on they decided to stay at home every time we went out to "claim" our house!

Nothing was going to stop us and we went anyway. We even lost some money in the process. On one occasion we saw an opportunity to "lease/purchase" a house. OH! We just knew that was it. We paid the one month's rent and security deposit on this house, in August, but the house wouldn't be available for us to move in until October. My wife stated; "Hun, this guy could be renting this house to us, and fifty other people. Well saints that proved to be a sure word from the Lord.

Approximately two weeks later our telephone rang. The caller explained that they were calling from the District Attorney's office and that we were victims of a crime. You guessed it, that property owner rented that building to guess how many people; yes you got it, **us and fifty other people!** Just like my wife had previously spoken. Yes, sometimes you will experience failure. We never, to this day got our money back.

On another occasion we lost a house which we had paid down on, trusted God for, and told everyone we were moving into, because we did not make the deadline for the balance owed. Although the owner verbally agreed to give us more time, she underhandedly sold it to another couple without informing us. The realtor was the one that finally informed us. Those experiences hurt!

Our children were right there praying and believing God with us.

Eventually the time came when we got the house God had for us, and believe me it was the perfect house for us. It was located just outside the city, about five minutes from our church, and had a very spacious backyard. This miracle came about in perfect timing. God made sure we did not get discouraged about coming up short every time, since by faith we kept telling the saints and our children that the Lord will provide soon.

Our failures taught us a valuable lesson. We saw in the scriptures many times when Jesus only took Peter, James, and John with him. (Matthew 9:25, Luke 9:28, Matthew 17:1, Mark5:37). The mistake we made before was that we kept telling other saints about "our house" that we just saw and "claimed." Just prior to the Lord granting us this miracle, we decided not to say a word to anyone- not even our own children. We kept that and did not reveal any information until after we signed the documents and got the keys.

That truly was a glorious day. This property owner was a saved woman of God. She had just lost her husband who died, and she was about to relocate. When she discovered that we were believers, were looking forward to purchasing our first house and that I had a degree from Temple University, she showed us great favor. She held the mortgage over the house, so that we didn't have to go to a bank, perform a credit check, etc. The sale was "by owner" so as such she could by-pass all those guidelines. God is so good! That miracle removed and replaced every feeling of defeat, discouragement or frustration.

While we were always telling the saints and non-believers about our faith in believing for a house, some of them stepped out in faith and got their houses even before we did. We rejoiced with them. They even shared with us that when we told them about our asking, seeking, and knocking principle, they got motivated and encouraged to do the same.

Remember those "failures" you read about earlier? We know that "All things work together for good, to them that love God, to them that are called according to His purpose". Later when we were purchasing our present church facility in 2001, appraised then at $1.5 million, we used the same principle, at first we told no one. It was only after that the sale was secured that we informed the congregation and others outside. The detail of how this was done will be explained later on in another chapter.

Again, the steps of faith sometimes include what I call failure. As previously mentioned, Abraham experienced this type of failure (delayed obedience) on his way to experiencing successful faith. With that said let us look at the steps of faith.

First failure (delayed obedience) of Abram

Genesis 12:1
Now the LORD had said unto Abram, Get thee out of thy country, and from thy kindred, and from thy father's house, unto a land that I will shew thee.

Remember, Abraham obeyed only one of the three commands God had given him– he left his own country. But he failed in obeying the last two. Instead of separating himself from his kindred, Terah his father and Lot his nephew, both went with him. Terah means "delay" and points to the fact that Abram"s family delayed his obedience to God's directive.

In fact, taking his family along against the wishes of God resulted in a "delay" of five years in Haran. Haran means "parched". Abram's response to God's call was partial and slow; and caused Abram to dwell in a "parch" place. In Isaiah 51:2, we learned that God called Abram "alone," not all his current family. Eventually in the end, he "obeyed." Heb. 11:8 said that "By faith Abram, when he was called to go out into a place which he should after receive for an inheritance, obeyed, and he went out, not knowing whither he went."

We are also called to **Separate ourselves** (see 1Corin. 6:15-20, 2Cor. 6:14-18, Is. 52:11-12). Abram's obedience in leaving Ur is thus singled out; but the Holy Ghost didn't mention him taking his "kindred" with him.

Success in Faith is obedience to God's Voice

Any step of faith should be made by using the Word of God as our foundation. Without the Word of God, there is literally no solid or sure foundation on which to stand. Romans 10:17 declares, **"So then faith cometh by hearing, and hearing by the Word of God."**

When operating by faith, on some occasion, immediate action is necessary. However, "Crazy Faith" does not mean we have to be in a hurry. Faith is willing to wait (see Is. 28:16; Heb. 6:12). Also, when moving by faith, we should remember that obedience to the Lord in spite of circumstances or consequences is a prerequisite (see Heb. 11:29-30).

Chapter 5
"Crazy Faith": The Joy of Breaking Down and Setting Up

As mentioned in a former chapter, when we were leaving our church members to establish a new ministry, we told them not to come with us. In an attempt to discourage any of them from joining our ministry we went across town in part to create a distance between us, and in part because we were to soon rent a more permanent space near the university. We rented a space from St. Joseph's University by exercising "Crazy Faith." Those early days provide memories that last a lifetime. Our sound system was a home tape deck that was far from being state of the art. We transported that in the trunk of my car, along with other things such as tapes and tambourines for our praise and worship.

Prayer, faith, and praise! Oh, we had church! Whenever one person would "wander in" we were elated with joy. If you wanted to find our location you had to try real hard. It was not easy to find us and we were almost hiding from the saints we knew. "Crazy Faith" requires you to look beyond your present circumstances yes, but it also requires some praise, joy, and appreciation just for who God is, not just for what He can give us. Our steadfastness continued week after week. We showed up and we still believed, sometimes not even knowing if anyone would show up through those doors. After spending 3 months renting space from St. Joseph's, we decided that we were not going to rent a more permanent space near the university that was being renovated for us to occupy. Instead, we moved the church into our home in Montgomery County. Oh! The joy of "breaking down and setting up" those folding metal chairs. Our Sunday mornings were spent like "nomads" going across town. Many who see us now have no idea where we came from.

While we were worshipping in our house in Cheltenham Township, a neighbor informed me that several other neighbors were complaining because of the "noise" we were making. Later, I discovered that he was the only one complaining. Even now in ministry when someone comes to me and says "others are saying", I stop them right there and request that they bring the "others" to see me. Most often I fail to see who the "others" are. In spite of that one person's complaint, God used it for His glory. It is then that we were prompted to start looking for a building to rent.

All through the scriptures, the enemy always tries to stop the work of the Lord. As children of God we have to be cognizant of this fact and do not "wither" under pressure from the enemy. We can use the Power of God against the enemy. Let's examine in Scripture how the Apostle Paul handled a similar situation.

Elymas the sorcerer was blinded immediately; because he tried to oppose Paul's preaching!

Acts 13:6-12
*⁶And when they had gone through the isle unto Paphos, they found a certain sorcerer, a false prophet, a Jew, whose name was Barjesus: ⁷Which was with the deputy of the country, Sergius Paulus, a prudent man; who called for Barnabas and Saul, and desired to hear the word of God. ⁸But Elymas the sorcerer (for so is his name by interpretation) withstood them, seeking to turn away the deputy from the faith. ⁹Then Saul, (who also is called Paul,) filled with the Holy Ghost, set his eyes on him, ¹⁰And said, O full of all subtilty and all mischief, thou child of the devil, thou enemy of all righteousness, wilt thou not cease to pervert the **right (lit., immediate)** ways of the Lord? ¹¹And now, behold, the **hand** of the Lord is upon thee, and thou shalt be blind, not seeing the sun for a season. And **immediately** there fell on him a mist and a darkness; and he went about seeking some to lead him by the hand. ¹²Then the deputy, when he saw what was done, believed, being astonished at the doctrine of the Lord.*

Sorcerers attempt to hinder the "**immediate** ways of the Lord" through their unlawful practices. However, we overcome them by flowing in the "immediacy" of the Lord Jesus through the "hand of the Lord" by the infilling of the Holy Spirit.

Be strong in the immediate faith of Jesus. Jesus is a "right now" Savior, Lord and King. He will move on your behalf "right now" if you ask from your heart and cry out to Him by prayer and fasting.

Chapter 6
"Crazy Faith": Seeing Through the Eyes of Faith

Another example of "Crazy Faith" occurred when we were looking for our first church building. My wife and I were simply looking for a building to rent. One day, as she was driving by on Cheltenham Avenue, she noticed a building for rent. Upon inquiring, the Real Estate Agent told us the adjacent building was for sale, but was not officially listed as such. He admonished us to "go for it". It' was "Crazy Faith" because we had no money in the bank, we did not have many members at the time, and we had just started as a congregation, hence no "track record" or history of good credit.

After seeing the building, we didn't move on it immediately. However, one day the realtor called out of the blue and said, "There's a lot of activity around the buying of the building. We quickly prayed, sought the Lord, and just believed God to step in. Our "Covering" literally "took a chance on us", and loaned us the money. But it should be known that someone else offered Ten Thousand Dollars ($10,000.00) more for the building; and was in a financial position to pay cash for the property. However, the testimony of the Real Estate Agent was that he thought the vision that we shared with him, (Equipping Believers to be Mighty Warriors who are living victoriously and demonstrating the courage to receive all God has for them, Spiritually, Emotionally, Physically, Socially, Financially and Intellectually), was more of what he wanted to see in that community. He just happened to live in that community.

The name of our Ministry is **Brand New Life Christian Center.** The name of the property then was "The Ivy Hill Bar." This was at that time, the most notorious bar in the city of Philadelphia. The then District Attorney had given the owners a choice; either they closed the bar or lose their license. They chose the former. This bar was the scene of murders, prostitution, fights, shootings, etc. The community wanted them gone. When we saw the building, the darkness, and the work that had to be done, we would have run away had it not been for "eyes of faith." God will give you glimpses of the potential He sees in a building, a person, an event, etc.

"Crazy Faith" produced "crazy results." Once again, a prospective buyer for the "Ivy Hill Bar", even though he produced $10,000.00 more in cash for the building, did not get it because God gave us favor, hence the start of "Brand New Life Christian Center's" stay in that facility was birthed. We now were serving "new wine" in that building, glory to God. At this point, we were only 7 months old as a congregation. We started in March of 1993 by renting a medium size banquet style room at St. Joseph's University on City Line Avenue in Philadelphia, and by operating in "Crazy Faith" 7 months later we we owned our first building!

"Crazy Faith" requires you to look beyond the present circumstances; as Abraham did in Romans 4:17-18, "As it is written, I have made thee a father of many nations before him whom he believed, even God, who quickeneth the dead, **and calleth those things which be not as though they were.** Who against hope believed in hope...." The situation in March 1993 when Brand New Life Christian Center was started as a Ministry was not very encouraging.

God has a secret to every blessing and sometimes we have to endure difficult situations for it to be revealed.

Hebrews 12:2-4 says:
*2 Looking unto Jesus the author and finisher of our faith; who for the joy that was set before him **endured** the cross, despising the shame, and is set down at the right hand of the throne of God. 3For consider him that endured such contradiction of sinners against himself, lest ye be wearied and faint in your minds. 4Ye have not yet resisted unto blood, striving against sin.*

Success in "Crazy Faith" is sometimes given only after a great struggle. If success was easy everyone would be successful. Success is only success because it relates to struggle. How can you have victory without conflict? To receive something without struggle lessens its own

33

personal value. Success is the reward that God gives to the diligent who, through perseverance, obtain the promise.

Hebrews 6:12-15
[12] *That ye be not slothful, but followers of them who through* **faith** *and* **patience** *inherit the promises.* [13] *For when God made promise to Abraham, because he could swear by no greater, he sware by himself,* [14]*Saying, Surely blessing I will bless thee, and multiplying I will multiply thee.* [15]*And so,* **after** *he had* **patiently endured,** *he obtained the promise.*

There is no way to perceive what God has for your life without fighting the obstacles and challenges that block your way to victory. Persevere and keep going. People are trying to find a way to reach the goal without going through the struggle.

Luke 14:28
"For which of you, intending to build a tower, sitteth not down first, and **counteth the cost,** *whether he have sufficient to finish it?"*

Luke indicated that "No man builds without counting the lost." There is a price to pay for every blessing. You must pay your price. Your payment helps you appreciate the blessings when they come, because you know the expense. You will not easily jeopardize something that was not easily attained.

Chapter 7
"Crazy Faith": Staying on The Wall (Working on the Building)

We actually physically occupied the Ivy Hill Bar facility for seven years from January 1994 to June 2001. The Ivy Hill Bar was located at 3218-20 W. Cheltenham Ave. in Philadelphia, PA. I could literally walk from my house in Laverock, Cheltenham Township to this facility. During these seven years at the Ivy Hill Bar, we often fasted, prayed, and sometimes spent all night in prayer.

We praised the Lord like never before and were enjoying the presence of the Holy Spirit. There were some saints that traveled from as far as Bear, Delaware, Chester, PA, and New Jersey. When they were asked why they tolerate the distance, their answer was; "A church alive is worth the drive." All I could say was "Hallelujah!"

I recently stopped by to say hello to the Pastor now occupying that facility. As I entered the building the memories came in quick succession. I could visualize all the fervent prayer meetings, the all night prayer, and the time spent repairing and renovating the building. I specifically remembered that as we initially labored, we wondered what we had gotten ourselves into. The first time I saw the inside of the building, it took a lot of restraint not to walk right out and forget about it. It was all black, dismal, dirty, and the odor was repulsive. So we pitched in, rolled up our sleeves, and went to work. A contractor did most of the heavy duty work and heating, ventilation, and air conditioning, while we did what we could to defray the cost. Once when we needed materials for the flooring we wondered where the extra finances would come.

At the same time, the contractor was starting to remove the paneling from the walls. We were all amazed when he realized that the wood paneling he was removing from the walls was the type that could be turned over and used for flooring material. God had already provided, and we didn't know it! Our first pews were given to us by Pastor Horace Shepherd Jr., Pastor of West Oak Lane Church of God. The colors fit perfectly with the wall colors that we already had in place.

One night after working until 2:00 AM, I shoveled my driveway removing a lot of snow. As I went back to my car to drive later that day I realized the township snow removal unit moved snow right back in front of my driveway. Completely, exhausted, I just left the car where it was and went to sleep!

The point here is that because we are operating by faith, it does not preclude us from hard work! Sometimes we will be physically exhausted, however faith without works is dead! Also, "Crazy Faith" requires works. Some of God's blessings are disguised as not worth the effort.

However, if we can see beyond that, the blessing will be manifested.

As we witnessed and won some to Christ, many of those saints joined us in working on the building. Some of the brethren that came from the homeless shelter became helpers in the house of God and provided significant contributions. Some even went on to become general contractors.

It is significant that faith is a part of the weapons of our warfare which God gives us to use to fight. We need the Shield of Faith to quench all the fiery darts of the wicked. *Ephesians 6:16 tells us:* *"Above all, taking the* *shield* *of faith, wherewith ye shall be able to quench all the fiery darts of the wicked".*

Faith is a shield, even risky faith. This type of "shield" was a great oblong shaped shield worn by the warrior to protect his body from the fiery darts thrown by the enemy. The darts were dipped in pitch or some combustible material and set on fire. When they struck, they served the purpose of a bomb.

Satan has his "fiery darts"—those things that have the potential to cause defeat, depression, discouragement (the "big 3"). Satan wants you to question your salvation, or calling. He wants you to doubt God, and to desire and lust after things that are not of God. He will lead you out of the will of God.

2 Chronicles 14:8

*And Asa had an army of three hundred thousand from Judah who carried **shields** and spears, and from Benjamin two hundred and eighty thousand men who carried shields and drew bows; all these were mighty men of valor.*

A shield is also defined as a "buckler," a defensive weapon! Goliath (a type of Satan) also had a shield. However, his shield was so large that it had to be carried by a shield, bearer. (1Sam. 17:7).

It is interesting to note that, the shields of Solomon (a type of Jesus) used 4 times as much gold as previously used (1Kings 10:16-17). This can mean that Jesus' shield of faith is reinforced with "glory" (one of the symbol of gold) to quench all the fiery dart of the devil. The armor of the believer is a spiritual armor—it is Christ. Satan in the book of Job (Job 1:10) says, "Hast not Thou made an hedge about him, and about his house, and about all that he hath on every side?"

Romans 13:12-14

*[12]The night is far spent, the day is at hand: let us therefore cast off the works of darkness, and let us **put on the armour of light.** [13]Let us walk honestly, as in the day; not in rioting and drunkenness, not in chambering and wantonness, not in strife and envying. [14]But **put ye on the Lord Jesus Christ,** and make not provision for the flesh, to fulfil the lusts thereof.*

As indicated above, Christ is also our armor. His armor is light, walking honestly, or orderly. The fiery darts of the wicked come fast and furiously. The only thing that will beat them down is the armor of Jesus, including but not limited to the shield of faith. We also have to stand in the midst of the fiery darts being thrown at us.

Ephesians 6:15
*Your **feet shod** with the **preparation** of the gospel of peace.*

Shoes are necessary for standing. They speak of the foundation. We need a good solid foundation and "preparation" is foundational. In combat, our feet must be anchored. That is we must stay in fellowship with your church, stop roaming all over! Jesus is our Rock!

Are your feet anchored on the Rock? The soldiers' shoes are not the dancing slippers of this world, or the slippers of the slothful, but the shoes of the warriors who knows Christ, and make Him known. Hold fast to the shield of faith and stand against all the fiery darts of the enemy. Put on the Lord Jesus Christ; take on the shield of faith.

Chapter 8
"Crazy Faith": Transitioning Into The Next Dimension

After being at the Ivy Hill Bar facility for a period of seven years, God blessed us, and allowed us to utilize every square foot of this facility. It was time to find a new facility. Our membership had increased, so we just needed more space.

"Crazy Faith" definitely requires some risk taking. Prior to us relocating, I felt the call to full-time ministry. At the time I was employed as a Director of Engineering. My wife was, and still is, a Speech Pathologist, and our tithing was the largest for our congregation. God has taught us the principle of tithing and we still do it today.

I remember the Sunday I announced from the pulpit that I was going into full time ministry, and consequently would be leaving my job. At that time I had a son who had just enrolled in college, and two daughters who were yet to enter college. To the natural mind, the logical thinking mind, the "sensible person", this makes no sense. As a matter of fact, that is why I use the term "Crazy Faith."

God wants us to trust Him only, to show our confidence in the Lord. Thank you Jesus! That Sunday morning after

I announced that I was going into ministry full time, by "taking a step of faith", I was joined in my office after service by a couple (who were at the time the second highest tithe payers). I thought they had come to see me, to offer some encouragement or a word from the Lord to confirm my actions. To my surprise, they told me that, that Sunday would be their last Sunday at Brand New Life Christian Center. Just like that, they had resigned from the congregation and taken their well-needed tithes with them.

As I sat in my chair, wondering, "What just happened?" I literally asked the Lord, "Are You sure about this full time Ministry stuff?"   After all, how was I going to explain this to my wife, children, Board of Elders and the congregation?   By the way, often times embarking on "Crazy Faith" leaves no logical explanation, things will sometimes get worse before they gets better.

Thank God, that risky step of faith was honored by the Lord. The congregation multiplied, and that one couple was replaced by several others. Today, all my children have graduated from college; my youngest daughter just received her Masters in Social Work from my Alma Mata, Temple University in Philadelphia, Pennsylvania.

Several Scriptures come to mind when discussing the subject of "Crazy Faith, which involves risk taking. For example, Moses' "Crazy Faith":

Hebrews 11:23-29:

[23]By faith Moses, when he was born, was hid three months of his parents, because they saw he was a proper child; and they were not afraid of the king's commandment. [24]By faith Moses, when he was come to years, refused to be called the son of Pharaoh's daughter; [25]Choosing rather to suffer affliction with the people of God, than to enjoy the pleasures of sin for a season; [26]Esteeming the reproach of Christ greater riches than the treasures in Egypt: for he had respect unto the recompence of the reward. [27]By faith he forsook Egypt, not fearing the wrath of the king: for he endured, as seeing him who is invisible. [28]Through faith he kept the passover, and the sprinkling of blood, lest he that destroyed the firstborn should touch them. [29]By faith they passed through the Red sea as by dry land: which the Egyptians assaying to do were drowned.

Why was Moses' faith covered in seven (7) verses? Moses received the most attention in the Hall of Faith (Heb. 11:4-9, 20-24, 30-31)! Why? I believe God knew that Moses had radical faith to perform radical things. Let's look at Moses, the Call of Moses, etc.

Moses was in the backside of the desert keeping the flock of Jethro, his father-in-law, when God's called came. A highly educated man, now he was occupied with one of the lowest positions ever. That should be enough to frustrate him and make him bitter. He was already used to the pleasures of the palace. Herding sheep was a profession held in very low esteem. He could have been feeling sorry for himself.

However, look at what happened to him in this place of humility. "And the angel of the Lord appeared unto him in a flame of fire out of the midst of a bush; and he looked, and behold, the bush burned with fire, and the bush was not consumed" (Exodus 3:2).

God told Moses in Exodus 3:8, "And I am come down to deliver them from the hands of the Egyptians and to bring them up out of that land...." Then in Exodus 3:10, God said: "Come now therefore, and I will send thee unto Pharaoh, that thou mayest bring forth my people ...." Exodus 3:11: "Moses said unto God, who am I, that I should go unto Pharaoh, and that I should bring forth the children of Israel out of Egypt?"

Exodus 4—**Look at verse 21:** "... see that thou do all those wonders before Pharaoh, which I have put into thine hand: **but I will** harden his heart, that he shall not let the people go." Can you hear (imagined what) Moses may have said in his mind—"What! You want me to go and tell him to let the people go, but You will harden his heart so he won't?" God said, yes!

Exodus 4:1-13 continued with Moses pleading with God saying he is not the one to go. In verse 2 Moses said: "And the Lord said unto him, what is that in thine hand? And he said a rod." However, in Exodus 4:19: "the Lord said unto Moses in Midian, go, return into Egypt." Finally in Exodus 4:20: "Moses took his wife and his sons ...and he returned to the land of Egypt. **And Moses took the rod of God in his hand.**" Read: Exodus 4:24-26. It is an awesome history!

The Lord (later) "met him and sought to kill him." Moses was so overwhelmed with mental distress or overtaken by a sudden and dangerous illness. Moses, during this time, had postponed or neglected the circumcision of one of his sons, probably the younger.

To do so was to break a covenant, and that was similar to a criminal offense in the Hebrew culture, especially a leader, destined by God as Moses was. Moses thought his sickness was a chastisement from the Lord for his neglecting to circumcise his son.

Concerned for her husband's safety, Zipporah overcame her maternal feelings of aversion to the painful ritual; she performed the circumcision herself, by using one of the sharp stones that she found in the desert (where she was at the time). Moses, who was supposed to do this, could not at the time. She explained to Moses that out of love for Moses, she had risked the life of her child. "So He (God) let him go." (Exodus 4:26) This means that Moses recovered. Then Moses enforced a faithful attention to this ritual of circumcision as a divine ordinance in Israel, it made their **peculiar distinction as a people.**

Chapter 9
"Crazy Faith": From "Serving New Wine" to "Raising the Dead"

After seven years at 3218-20 W. Cheltenham Ave (The Ivy Hill Bar facility where we served "new wine"), it was now time to move, pull up stakes, and find a new facility with more space. We were looking at a building adjacent to our present location. The problem was there was literally no parking, and while we could still use our current building also for the sanctuary, Sunday School, etc., the space problem was still a big issue.

However, we were desperate, so we moved ahead and paid a deposit on this building. The day prior to the settlement, a friend in ministry called me to inform me that a bigger building in the city was now available, and the wonderful thing about this facility was, it had more than adequate parking and space to really expand.

My wife and I quickly arranged to see this building, without telling anyone anything. We met with the Real Estate Agent at this recently discovered property. As we toured the building, and the Real Estate Agent turned on a set of chandeliers that occupied a long hallway, I distinctly heard the voice of the Holy Spirit said, "This is it!" I immediately shouted, "Hallelujah, Jesus!" Remember, we learned our lesson from the experience of failure when we were trying to purchase our first house.

We kept this confidential, and prayed for God's perfect will to be manifested. I actually gave God something like a "fleece". I said to the Lord, that if this was His will for us to have this spacious, well-kept facility, then He would have to stop the settlement scheduled for the next day on the property adjacent to 3218-20 W. Cheltenham Ave. A security deposit was already placed on that property. Legally we could not be refunded the deposit if we decided on the last day prior to the settlement date to withdraw.

Miraculously, two series of events occurred at the "ninth hour". On the very day of the settlement, that morning just as I was about to go downtown in Philadelphia for the scheduled settlement, I received a telephone call from the seller's representative informing me that the settlement had to be cancelled. Two reasons were given. First, the Real Estate representative had lost the check fot the security deposit, and second, the building we were about to purchase had three liens that were not discovered earlier. Basically, we were out of that commitment.

I said, "Thank you Jesus," and instantly started to praise the Lord. The lady on the other end of the telephone asked me if I was O.K., I assured her I was, told her thank you, got off the phone. I told my wife what just happened, then we both celebrated. God had just answered our prayer. We knew "it was already done".

Keep in mind that "Crazy Faith" is not crazy, but it does involve a very high degree of trust in the Lord, and a willingness to "risk it all." More importantly, God's perfect will for our lives is much more rewarding than His permissive will.

Actually, the events leading up to possessing this newly found facility illustrated **that "Crazy Faith"** is not **"crazy"**. Some thought, planning, analysis, demographic study, feasibility study, collaborations with other Pastors, and seeking wise counsel (remember in the multitude of counsel there is safety), were all part of the decision, along with some "common sense" and prudent actions.

It would be misleading to have anyone believing that the topic of this book, "Crazy Faith" is recommending reckless behavior, or irresponsible behavior that has no Biblical foundation, or completely disregard for sound wisdom. On the contrary, the writer believes, "Wisdom is the principal thing, therefore **get wisdom,** and with all thy getting **get understanding."** I sincerely want to emphasize this point because, as a Pastor, I have seen people do some "strange things" in the name of stepping out in faith.

I believe, first, one needs a word from the Lord-some Biblical basis as a foundation to stand on. Coupled with this, prayer and obedience should accompany your faith walk. So, please do not be misled by the title. There are instances where the Lord literally shows us mercy and grace and actually comes to our rescue. Consequently, how the Lord leads one person cannot be used as a "blueprint" to suggest this is the way God works all the time.

The new facility we were believing God for was the Kirk and Nice Funeral Home, which was the oldest funeral home in the country. It was built in 1761; This spacious three story facility occupies 1.14 acres. We often tell others, "We now raise the dead."

The purpose of this book is to outline some series of events as it happened in my life, simply to encourage you to continue in the things of Christ Jesus. This is how the Lord led my wife and I; with you He might choose a different series of events. However, His principles are the same.

So, what happened next? The Lord stopped the settlement, and we told no one, literally, no one. We started fasting and praying, I started a teaching series on faith in our congregation for about three months. The church knew that the building next door had a problem with the liens, so we were not moving in that direction anymore.

One of my Pastor friends told me he thought the expenses that would be needed to keep and occupy that new facility (The Kirk and Nice building), would be too much for our then, one-hundred member congregation. We "crunched" the numbers (did the math); it just could not add up. I went back to God. I said, "Lord, You heard what my colleague in the ministry said. He told me you (Earl Palmer) can't do this". To my surprise, the Lord answered me in a way that initially left me rather stunned.

I heard the Holy Spirit said, "He's right, you cannot do this." I was ready to react but I kept quiet for further instructions. Then I heard, "But I can do this; for with God, all things are possible. Also, I can do all things through Christ who strengthens me." I got my "Word" from the Lord. We later informed our Board of Elders, next our leaders and finally the congregation.

Another miracle happened next. The facility, "The Kirk and Nice Funeral Home", located at 6301 Germantown Avenue, was appraised in 2001 at 1.5 Million Dollars. Now you should understand why the title of this book is "Crazy Faith". First, we were currently occupying a "store front building", the "Ivy Hill Bar" (where we served new wine), and now we want to purchase a building worth 1.5 Million Dollars! Some intermediary step, logically speaking, should be next. Who moves from a storefront with approximately one hundred people, to a facility that is worth that much? That was not the recommended sequence. Secondly, where was the money to pay for this building?

God performed one miracle after another. He had "a ram in the bush". In our corporate headquarters, at the time, I spoke to several people about our vision and intentions. One of those individuals was Dr. Michael Curry, who was in a very influential position in the Church of God in Anderson, Indiana.

After hearing my vision, he flew to Philadelphia on a Memorial Day weekend and toured the facility we wanted to purchase. I afterwards referred to Dr. Curry as a "Joseph in Egypt" (he remains one of my best friends in the Ministry today)! From that day on he worked with us. We were able to finance the mortgage through the Church of God in Anderson, Indiana.

Other persons that labored with us during this time were Dr. Charles Shumate, Faith Phile, from the church of God in Anderson, Indiana, Reverend O'Conner from New Jersey, and Dr. Milton C. Grannum from New Covenant Church of Philadelphia.

God has a sense of humor! We moved from "serving new wine" at the Ivy Hill Bar, to now, "raising the dead" at the previous "Kirk and Nice Funeral Home". Our membership grew significantly once we moved. We were not taking that factor into account in our calculations. God knew all along.

Lastly, concerning personal testimonies, when dealing with what I call "Crazy Faith". The Lord had placed a burden in my heart in regards to planting a church in Jamaica. I shared it with my wife, Maria, my children, Joshua, Rebecca and Rachel, afterwards with the Elders, Leaders and members of Brand New Life Christian Center.

Initially, I met with the executive committee of the Church of God in Jamaica. During that meeting I was asked, "Why plant a church in Jamaica?" I told them what I could, shared some things that had occurred in my life, and the fact that I wanted to make some significant positive contribution to Jamaica, since I was born and raised in Jamaica,

Also, I shared with them that once I left my Great-Aunt's house (who raised me), I never went back to say thank you. After all that, the recurring question was, "Who is going to be the Pastor of this congregation in Jamaica?" Everyone was asking the same question. I literally had no reasonable answer.

As time went on, we started the congregation in March of 2010. Two of the Pastors that were in that meeting in Jamaica, Pastor Courtney Gordon and Pastor Dexter Johnson, actually spoke on our behalf and went beyond that by coordinating their efforts to take turns preaching at the newly formed Brand New Life Church of God, Jamaica. The Executive Chairman, Rev. Dr. Lenworth

Anglin was very supportive and instrumental in "grafting" us in and encouraging the Pastors to support us. Just recently, the Lord set aside a couple that will be trained to eventually assume leadership of this congregation.

Chapter 10
"Crazy Faith": A Miracle: With God All Things Are Possible

As we continue to discuss the subject of "Crazy Faith", it is imperative that we understand that the grace of God on numerous occasions literally rescues us from our human failures and shortcomings. Please do not ascribe to any man the glory that belongs to the Lord Jesus Christ. To Him, be all the glory, honor, and praise! So let's be clear- it is not that the writer possesses any "extra measure of faith" than anyone else.

On the contrary, as the word tells us, every man possesses a certain measure of faith. Now, we know the word also declares that "not all men have faith", that is not every man exercises the measure of faith given to them. So then, faith without works is dead.

It all started on May 22nd, 2006 after I'd just been through what I thought was a routine colonoscopy. As I waited on the doctor in the recovery room I couldn't help but notice his somber attitude as he entered the room. This was not my first colonoscopy procedure. During a prior one I recalled he was talkative, jovial, and a complete reversal of his present state. I started the conversation "Hi doc, how does it look?" "Not good" was his reply as he advised me to call my wife who was waiting in the lobby to drive me home. When she came in the room the doctor told us his findings. "Well, he said, you have a tumor in the rectal area; the largest one I've ever seen. We can try chemotherapy, but first I'd like you to see a surgeon."

It is always much easier to talk about faith when you are not going through anything. However, when you are in the middle of the fire, it's a completely different situation. I remember sitting in that waiting room staring at the doctor and hoping he had made a mistake, as my wife began to speak the word; "We trust the Lord, and He can work it out." Those words transferred the thoughts in my mind from the shocking news I just heard.

Immediately I prayed in my heart, "Lord I need your help now."We listened to the doctor's recommendation. I went to see another doctor at the University of Pennsylvania Hospital, after that a visit to Thomas Jefferson Hospital, and next to Chestnut Hill Hospital where they scheduled me for chemotherapy and radiation. One of my doctors from the University of Pennsylvania Hospital told me that the tumor although very large, had not penetrated the membrane walls, which was a positive sign.

As it so happened, a day prior to my scheduled radiation treatment I met with the surgeon. She inquired about my results from the lab and was quite concerned that they had not been reviewed before issuing treatment for chemotherapy and radiation. I will never forget that phone call from her. "Reverend Palmer, she said, It is not cancer." When the doctor at the colonoscopy center made his initial diagnosis, he told me he was sure it was cancer. The latest news from the surgeon was truly an answer to my prayer. An important principle should be re-iterated here.

After learning about this rectal tumor, I met with my family, that is my wife and three children. Each one prayed as we held hands in a circle. We did not tell anybody else about this. We have learned over the years (remember our attempts of purchasing our first house) that not everyone that "says" they agree with you, actually does.

Next, the chemotherapy and radiation treatment were cancelled, and a surgery date was scheduled for June 14th, 2006. The surgeon explained that she would try the Flex Sigmoid Oscopy method. If successful then she would not have to open the abdomen. The Lord moved miraculously, and the operation was indeed successful.

There was no trace of cancer, and the tumor was removed. The nurses and doctors of Chestnut Hill Hospital told me that my hospitalization was the fastest recovery they have ever seen! After surgery I was discharged in four days. Glory to God for that time of miraculous healing! As I am presently writing this book, a few days ago I had another routine colonoscopy and received "a clean bill of health." God is indeed good!

Afterwards I visited my primary physician, for my yearly physical examination. At the conclusion of this examination, I requested the documentation of the specifics of the operation performed on June 14, 2006. The procedure performed included "laparoscopic – assisted low interior resection with diverting ostomy".

As I read through the details of the operation performed, I cannot help but to give God praise for His wondrous works. We are indeed fearfully and wonderfully made. I thank the Lord for His guidance and protection during and after the operation. I thank God for the doctors, nurses, and all the medical team that had a part in my operation.

God gives us special favor, even concerning our health. Psalm 102:13-18 says: *"Thou shalt arise, and have mercy upon Zion: for the time to favour her, yea, the set time, is come. 14For thy servants take pleasure in her stones, and favour the dust thereof. 15 So the heathen shall fear the name of the LORD, and all the kings of the earth thy glory. 16 When the LORD shall build up Zion, he shall appear in his glory. 17He will regard the prayer of the destitute, and not despise their prayer. 18This shall be written for the generation to come: and the people which shall be created shall praise the LORD."*

Favor—"Yea, the set time is come ... when the Lord shall build up Zion...." **Zion** is the Church! We are that generation to come that the Lord will favor. As the Psalmist said, "This shall be written for **the generation to come!**" We are the forty second generation of Christ. This is the set time for the favor of Jesus upon His generation in this age!

There is the favor of God to heal **"right now."** In Acts 14:8-10 there was a "... cripple who never had walked, Paul perceiving that he had faith to be healed declared that the man should stand up and be healed. The man walked immediately! It won't work for us if we break spiritual **rules!**

We must obey the word! Immediate faith must be exercised; Acts 10:44, "While Peter yet spake these words..." Isaiah 65:24, "Before they call I will answer..." Right now faith; faith for immediate results, immediate faith brings immediate results.

The Right Now Faith of Jesus:

John 11:1-5
Now a certain man was sick, named Lazarus, of Bethany, the town of Mary and her sister Martha. *2 (It was that Mary which anointed the Lord with ointment, and wiped his feet with her hair, whose brother Lazarus was sick.)* *3 Therefore his sisters sent unto him, saying, Lord, behold, he whom thou lovest is sick.* *4 When Jesus heard that, he*

said, This sickness is not unto death, but for the glory of God, that the Son of God might be glorified thereby.

John 11:21-23
*²¹Then said Martha unto Jesus, Lord, if thou hadst been here, my brother had not died. ²² But I know, that even **now,** whatsoever thou wilt ask of God, God will give it thee. ²³ Jesus saith unto her, Thy brother shall rise again.*

Jesus said: "This sickness is not unto death, but for the glory of God, that the Son of God might be glorified thereby." (John 11:14-15), "...Nevertheless let us go unto Him." (John 11:17, 20-23); "Then said Martha unto Jesus, Lord..." (John 11:22); "But I know that even **now,** whatever thou wilt ask of God, God will give it thee." (John 11:23).

"Jesus saith unto her, Thy brother shall rise again." (John 11:39); Jesus said, "**You**" take away the stone. Something's **"we"** have to do, we have our responsibility to live holy, to walk uprightly; etc. (John 11:39), "Martha, **saith** unto Him, Lord, by this time he stinketh: for he hath been dead four days." (John 11:40), "Jesus **saith** unto her, said I not unto thee, that if thou wouldest **believe,** thou shouldest **see** the glory of God?

John 11:43-45
⁴³And when he thus had spoken, he cried with a loud voice, Lazarus, come forth. ⁴⁴And he that was dead came forth, bound hand and foot with graveclothes: and his face

was bound about with a napkin. Jesus saith unto them, Loose him, and let him go. ⁴⁵ *Then many of the Jews which came to Mary, and had seen the things which Jesus did, believed on him.*

Chapter 11
"Crazy Faith": Never Forget Where You Come From

As you may recall, I was raised by my Great Aunt, "Aunt G". She was a Godly woman; so consequently, I had to go to church every Sunday, even though I had to walk approximately two miles up a steep hill. Of course I had to make it in time for Sunday school and stay until the entire church service was over.

It was in Sunday School that I learned about Jesus. As I grew older I made an oath to myself that as soon as I left that house, I would never step foot in another church. Yes, I meant every word. "Mommy" as I called her, made it crystal clear at the time that if I didn't go to church then I would not be eating in her house. At the time I went because I had no choice. Furthermore, I personally disdained the preachers at that church. They would preach to me on Sundays, but during the week as I hitchhiked to school, I never once got a ride from any of them. So, I grew up with the mentality that all preachers are "fake".

After graduating from High School (Mannings High, in Savanna-La-Mar), I immediately left the Parrish of Westmoreland, and went to the city of Kingston to live. I was born in Kingston, Jamaica; and was given to my

Great Aunt in the rural area (Westmoreland) to care for me from a baby. As I later discovered I was left on the steps of my father's house (while he was at work). His neighbors took me in until he came home later from work. When God has a purpose for your life, the enemy cannot stop God's destiny for you! God used my Great Aunt to nurture me, and demonstrate the love of God in a real and tangible way.

However, as I moved to Kingston, one thing was sure, as far as I was concerned, there would be no more church for me. I immediately got a job as a television cameraman at the only T.V. station at the time, Jamaica Broadcasting Corporation. While working there I took an electrical engineering course at the College of Arts, Science and Technology (CAST) and a Zoology course at the University of the West Indies. I was still highly motivated and searching for my niche in life.

The sad truth is that once I left my house in Water Works in Westmoreland, Jamaica, I never once called or went back to see my Great Aunt - something I regret until this day! When she passed I didn't even know; I found out afterwards. In 1984, years later after I had immigrated to the United States (1974), I went back to Jamaica. After visiting my Great Aunt's grave, and repenting to the Lord for not seeing her prior to her death, it was then that I was burdened to start a church in Jamaica- to give back to the land of my birth.

My first visit back to Water Works where I grew-up, brought back "memories that last a lifetime". I distinctively remembered as a little boy standing on a hill overlooking the district, and praying to God asking Him "Please just let me get to America". I believed even then, that I just had to get to the "states"; my destiny was tied into "coming to America". Looking back now I can see that.

Where I grew-up was in the hills, a place named, "Abeokuta", and I was so ashamed as a little boy to tell others where I was from. It was located up on top of a hill, above an ice factory, and above the river. Few people would visit this area. Cars, literally struggled to get up there, because the hill was so steep! In these early days of my childhood, I didn't wear shoes, and going barefoot was normal. I even walked miles to school in my barefeet. As a young boy, I stammered a lot, and the words took a long time before finally coming out.

I was constantly ridiculed because of my speech impediment. Coupled with this, I was known to have several attacks of epilepsy. This was a violent type of seizure that would leave me motionless after several minutes. On more than one occasion, this seizure occurred while I was at the edge of the river. I thank God for His mercy and His grace.

Being rejected by my mother and father, and for the most part, my whole family was very difficult for me when I was growing up. I struggled with rejection, which I believe prompted me to excel in school and whatever I did. I was trying to find acceptance. Jamaica is not really known for color prejudice, but class prejudice, which is just as bad if not worse. At that time there were only two groups or "classes" in Jamaica; those who had money and those who didn't. There were no middle classes. Oh! You knew early in life which "side of the fence you belonged on". So, I grew-up with an inferiority complex, and a spirit of rejection that led to bitterness and resentment. I was clearly "the black sheep" of the family. Born "out of wed-lock", certainly did not help the situation.

Some memories cause me to laugh out loud now. For example, once they took a photograph of me, and hid my feet behind some bushes because I didn't have any shoes. I was standing beside my cousin who had on shoes, and the picture was going to his mother who lived in England. My Great Aunt insisted that I should be in the picture, so hiding my feet was the answer. Real funny; they meant well.

Why share all of these embarrassing details? And what do they have to do with anything? To show that our past doesn't matter to God. Yes, He does choose the foolish things of this world to confound the wise. Also, to show that in order for us to operate in faith, we must trust

God. The spirit of rejection and hurt can often hinder our ability to trust God. We need divine healing in these areas.

In 1974 when I immigrated to the United States, I was attending Boston University when I began to be homesick. I started praying for the first time. I asked God for two things. First, I asked God if He was real to reveal Himself to me. Second, I asked God for a wife. Yes, I was lonely! God answered both prayers. I will never forget coming to Philadelphia for a Thanksgiving Holiday visit.

One of my friends, Dwight Morrison, had a surprise party waiting for me. As I walked in that house, on that cold winter night, some of my high school friends from Mannings High, in Westmoreland, Jamaica were at the party. Dwight had secretly arranged this surprise. It was truly great; I didn't want this time to pass. I rescheduled my trip back to Boston once, and had it not been for college would have rescheduled again.

On the train ride back to Boston, I got on in Philadelphia, and on that train I met a beautiful young lady, who was leaving and returning to her apartment in New York. It just so happened that she lived very close to my father's house in the Bronx. So, when I came to New York for Christmas Holiday, you guessed it, I went to visit her. Her name then was Maria Robinson. Today she is my wife. We were married on March 29, 1975, four months after we met. On June 15th, 1975, I accepted Jesus Christ as my personal Lord and Savior. My wife accepted Christ three weeks later. God answered both prayer requests.

As I am finishing this book, I just received news that my father went home to be with the Lord on December 27, 2011. I led him to Christ quite a few years ago. God is so good! He uses past experiences to help shape our future purpose and destiny. This is just an attempt to illustrate how the Lord has led me, and used me especially in the realm of faith and deliverance. But I had to be a first partaker of His grace, mercy, and deliverance. To God be the all the glory, honor and praise.

Jeremiah 29:11 says, *"For I know the thoughts that I think towards you, saith the Lord, thoughts of peace and not of evil, to give you an expected end."*

Throughout our journey in life, we may be faced with many obstacles and afflictions. Sometimes we believe these struggles to be either punishment from God, or self-afflicted. Moreover, in spite of the cause we should rest assured in knowing that God has a purpose and plan for our lives. Even when our lives take a detour, God still has the power to turn those situations into good. Remember that regardless of your circumstances, God will get the glory out of your life!

Be blessed!

About the Author

Pastor Earl F. Palmer is a native of Jamaica, West Indies. He immigrated to the United States in August 1974 where he met and married his wife Maria in 1975. Pastor Earl Palmer and his wife, Pastor Maria R. Palmer, are the Pastors of Brand New Life Christian Center, in Philadelphia, Pennsylvania, which they founded in March of 1993. Pastor Palmer has an apostolic anointing and as such oversees other churches beyond the Philadelphia are, namely, Norristown, PA; Baltimore, MD; and Mandeville in Jamaica. In March of 2010, Brand New Life Church of God, Jamaica was launched in Kingston, Jamaica. Pastor Palmer holds a Bachelor of Science degree in Mechanical Engineering. He has attended Jamison Bible Institute, The Center for Urban Theological Studies, Christian Research and Development Institute, and Covenant International Institute. He has also earned an advanced ETA Certificate. He and his wife, Maria are blessed with one son, Joshua and two daughters, Rebecca and Rachel.

Contact Information
Pastors Earl and Maria Palmer
Brand New Life Christian Center
6301 Germantown Ave
Philadelphia, PA 19144
Email: manofgod1124@verizon.net